How to Start Your Own Lemonade Business

by

DJ Parry

Dedicated to Davis the Step-Dog,

who taught me more about making lemonade from lemons than

anyone else ever could have.

Table of Contents

Notes to the Parents:

Congratulations! You have made a wise decision! By buying this book for your children, you have begun the process of developing their creativity and resourcefulness. You have just provided them with a road map that will guide them, not only in this venture, but in many other projects that they will tackle throughout their lives.

Who can pass up cold lemonade on a hot day? Certainly not this writer, especially if the entrepreneurs happen to be kids. This little how-to book will teach your kids, step by step, how to start their own lemonade business. It is designed to be read and followed by the kids themselves-helping them not only to develop self-confidence and ambition, but also helping them to develop the ever important skill of following instructions.

Your guidance from a distance will be helpful, but for the most benefit, let the kids do as much of the process themselves as they possibly can. They will become little businesspeople. They will learn that with a little effort and a lot of creativity, they can profit from their labors. They will learn basic concepts about business, such as planning, building, advertising, customer service, money handling, and the importance of location. Of course, they won't realize they're learning. They'll just know that they're having fun and earning some extra money.

This book will serve only as a guide. It will provide a lot of suggestions, along with lots of opportunities for decisions to be made. It will be up to your children to figure out exactly what they want their stand to look like, what kind of lemonade they want to sell, where they want to locate, and how they want to advertise. The book emphasizes that they should always get permission from you, the parents. It also emphasizes the importance of cleaning up after themselves.

So, as the parent, try to oversee without interfering. Remember that one purpose of the adventure is to let your child see why he or she should do things a certain way and how it's going to benefit him or her in the long run. The results will be a happy kid with a basic understanding of how a business works.

List of Possible Materials Needed:

(REMEMBER THAT THE LIST DEPENDS ON WHAT <u>YOU</u> WANT.)

1) Stuff needed to build the Lemonade Stand:
        Boards, Nails, and Hammer
                or
        Card Table
                or
        Cardboard Boxes
                or
        Boxes to set a board across

        Spray Paint

        Shelf Liner or a Table Cloth

2) Stuff needed to make the Lemonade:
        A pitcher
        Lemons
        Water
        Ice
        Sugar
                or
        Lemonade-flavored Kool-Aid
                or
        Frozen Lemonade

3) Stuff needed to make the Signs:
        Poster board or Cardboard
        Magic Markers or something to write with
        Streamers or Flags

4) Other stuff you may need:
        Ice chest
        Cups
        A lemon juicer
        A grater or potato peeler
        Grape juice or beet juice
        A box to keep your money in
        Chairs
        Paper for flyers (Advertising signs)

Introduction

Did you know that every year August 20th is designated as "National Lemonade Day"? Did you know that several cities also designate certain days each year as "National Lemonade Stand Day"? It's true.

National Lemonade Stand Day began unofficially in 2000 when a little four-year-old girl named Alexandra "Alex" Scott set up a lemonade stand to raise money to help kids with cancer. Alex herself had cancer. It was her way of doing what she could to help others. Her idea caught on and soon there were hundreds of lemonade stands all over the United States, raising money to help kids with cancer and to fund research which one day will find a cure.

The dates of National Lemonade Stand Day vary city by city, so if you want to participate, you'll need to check with your city officials or on the internet to find out what day it will be held in your town. If the idea hasn't made it to your area yet, why not start a National Lemonade Stand Day campaign and get it going in your hometown! It's a fun way to help others.

Now, let's learn how to start a lemonade business!

CHAPTER ONE: PLANNING YOUR BUSINESS

Okay, kids, there are a few things you need to think about before you get started on building your stand and making your lemonade. Planning is always a fun step and lets you work out all the details before you actually start building. It can save you a lot of time in the long run.

First of all, you need to decide where you want to locate the stand. Do you want to put it in your own front yard, or is your neighbor's yard a better location? Or, perhaps you may want to set it up at a local park or ball field. Or, maybe your grandparents have a good spot. You'll need to think about how many potential customers you'll get at each location. You'll also need to think about how safe the location would be for both you and your customers. You will want to choose a safe place. You don't want your customers to have to cross a busy street to get to your stand. And, very importantly, you'll need to get permission wherever you choose to put it. Explain what you're doing and where you'll be, and make sure it's okay with the people who own the property.

Then you need to decide what kind of stand you want to have. Do you want a big one or a small one? Do you want it to be really fancy or just simple? Do you want to have some chairs out in front of it, so that your customers can sit down to enjoy their lemonade? A good way to design your stand is just to sit down with a pencil and piece of paper and draw a picture of what you want the stand to look like.

Next, you'll have to decide what kind of lemonade you'll want to sell. Do you want to have old-fashioned, fresh-squeezed lemonade, or do you want to use frozen lemonade? What about "pink" lemonade? You could also consider lemonade-flavored Kool-Aid. You'll need to think about what size of cup you want to sell. Will you have more than one size? And do you want to sell other things at your stand, such as cookies or popcorn?

What days do you want to have your stand open—every day or just on the weekends? Or, maybe you want to just have the stand open in the hot afternoons when people will be thirsty. Or, maybe you want to take weekends off! It's all up to you.

How do you plan to get customers? Are you going to put up signs around the neighborhood, or are you just going to have your friends telling people about your stand? There are a lot of ways to let people know about your business. Later on in this book, you'll learn different ways to advertise for free.

Next, you'll need to figure out where you'll get the materials for your stand and the stuff you'll need for the lemonade. Your parents or friends may be able to help you out. Usually, if you explain what you're doing, they'll be happy to give you something. If not, you may need to buy what you'll need to get started.

How are you going to keep track of the money you make? What will you keep the money in? Are you going to have a helper that you will be sharing the money with? Will you have kids who work for you? If so, how much will you pay them? Or, are you going to do the project by yourself and keep all the money you make?

One last thing you'll need to think about is a name for your business. Perhaps you can call it "Lenny's Lemonade" (if your name is Lenny) or "Lori's Lemons" (if your name is Lori) or "Mike's Terrific Lemonade" (if your name is Mike). Or maybe something simple like "Stop-n-Sip." It's up to you!

So, let's get started! There's a lot of fun to be had and some extra spending money to be made!

CHAPTER TWO: LOCATION, LOCATION!

So, have you decided where you want to set up your stand? That's something that you should probably be sure about before you start to build it. Of course, if you decide to move it, you can always do that too. Remember, though, if you think you'll be moving it around a lot, you may want to take that into consideration when you are building it. It's easier to move something in several parts than to try to move a big one-piece stand.

The location is very important! You want a place where you'll get a lot of customers coming by. Sometimes a corner location is good! Sometimes a spot under a big shady tree is good. Customers like to drink lemonade in the shade. Maybe a spot next to a bus stop would be good. Just always make sure that your parents know where you are.

If you have decided to put your stand in your front yard, which is where most stands are located, then the first thing you need to do is to ask permission from your parents to make sure that it's okay with them. They probably won't care, as long as you keep the area cleaned up. No one wants a lot of trash blowing around in their yard. Just keep a small trash can or cardboard box handy for your customers to put their used cups in.

If you have decided that you would get more business if you set your stand up in a neighbor's yard, then be sure to ask your neighbor and your parents if that is okay. Be sure to tell your neighbor that you'll keep the site clean and then be sure to keep it clean! Always do what you say you'll do! That way, they'll trust you and know that you keep your word.

If you decide to set up your stand at a local park, make sure that your City allows it. Just call City Hall and ask them. Or, if you prefer, have your parents call them. Usually, the City won't mind, but sometimes they have certain rules that they have to follow. A local park can be a good location if the park has a lot of visitors.

Another good location might be near an office building. Be sure to let the people inside the office know that your stand is there. That way, when the people working there get a break, they can go outside and buy a lemonade from you. Once again, be sure it's okay to locate there.

If there's a nearby baseball field, you might want to think about setting your stand up close to it to sell cold lemonade to the players. If there are games going on, there's the opportunity for even more business, especially if there isn't a concession stand already there. If there is a concession stand, they may not allow you to sell inside the ballpark. In that instance, you might be able to locate just outside the gates and sell to people as they go in or come out.

Keep in mind that if you locate your stand somewhere other than close to home, you'll need to think about how you're going to get there and how you'll keep your lemonade cold while you're there.

As you can see, location can be very important. If you're on a dead-end street that doesn't have any cars or people go down it, you're not going to get much business. So, be picky! The better the location, the better your business will be!!!!

CHAPTER THREE: BUILDING THE STAND

Okay, you've got your location picked out and you've asked permission to set up your stand there. Now you're ready to build the stand! The fun part!!!!

Your stand can be as plain and simple as you want, or it can be as fancy and professional as you want. It all depends on how much work you want to put into building it and what kind of materials you have to build it with. Remember, it's not the stand you're selling. You don't need to go out and buy a lot of materials to build the stand......just use what you already have!

Let's start out with a very simple stand. All you need is a cardboard box! That's right.....just something to set the lemonade on. Make sure the bottom of the box is solid. If it's not, use some duct tape to tape it together, so that it will be sturdy. Then turn the box upside down, so that the bottom of it becomes the top. Then it's a table. If you don't think it's going to be sturdy enough to hold the lemonade pitcher and glasses or cups, then you can always set a flat board across the top of it. Make sure the top of your box (table) is clean. You can use a towel or a tablecloth to cover it, or you can use some peel-and-stick shelf liner, if you have it. Then, you can decorate the box if you want to. Plain, simple, easy to make!

Okay, if you want to make a little larger stand, it's very easy to do, also. Just get two cardboards boxes and a board that is three or four feet long. Turn the boxes upside down and place them two or three feet apart. Then lay the board across the top of the boxes, making a long table. If your boxes are sturdy, you should have a fairly sturdy stand. If they're not sturdy, then you need to either tape them to make them sturdy, or get some different boxes. Be sure that if you make the two-box stand, that the boxes are approximately the same size, or at least the same height. If they are not, your board will not be level. You want to have a nice level top, so that your lemonade will not spill. Again, you can cover the top with anything you want, as long as it is clean and smooth.

Another easy way to make a lemonade stand is to use a card table. Just unfold the legs and make sure they're locked into place. Then, you're in business! Keep the top of the table clean. You can always cover it with a small tablecloth or a towel. Always make sure that your folks say it is okay to use the table and tablecloth or whatever it is you decide to use.

If you want to actually build a stand, you can do that, too. Remember, though, that you probably won't be able to move it as easily as you can move the stands that I have described above. However, a well-built stand can last for a long time. Here are some easy-to-follow instructions for a custom-built stand. Remember that you can always change it to fit your own design.

The base of the stand will have a front, a top and two ends on it. If you want, you can also put a back on it, but the back isn't necessary. First of all, you'll need to build a frame. Follow the numbered pictures here to see how you need to put it together. You can always make it bigger or smaller than these measurements, if you want. These sizes are for an average-sized stand. For the frame, you'll need four (4) 2x4s, each about four feet long, four (4) 2x4s about two-and-a-half feet long, and four (4) 2x4s about two feet long. (A 2x4 is a board that is about 2 inches thick and about 4 inches wide. It can be any length.) Be sure to get permission before cutting up any boards. And, always, always, get permission before using any of your parents' tools. You can cut the boards with a hand saw, if you like, but be sure to have your parents watch you as you saw the wood. If you want your parents to help you, just ask them. I'm sure they'll be more than happy to help. If they have an electric saw, they can cut the wood for you a lot faster than you can cut it by hand. However, never, never, never use an electric saw yourself. Electric saws can be very dangerous and shouldn't be used by young people. If you want to cut the wood yourself, you can do it with a hand saw. You'll still need to be careful, but a hand saw is much safer to use than an electric saw.

Okay, place two of the 4' long 2x4s and two of the 2 ½' long 2x4s in a rectangle as shown in Figure 1. Be sure to put the shorter ends (the 2 ½' pieces) inside the longer pieces, so that the longer boards are on the outside of the shorter boards. Now, nail the pieces together as shown.

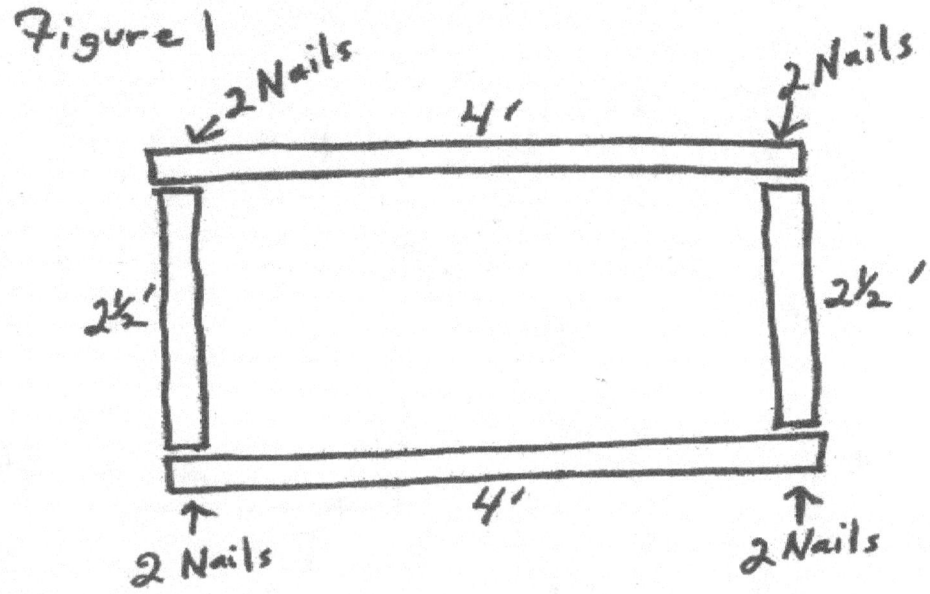

Figure 1

Make sure the nails are at least 4" long, so that they will go through the flat side of the 2x4s and still have enough nail to go deep into the bottom board. If your nails are too short, they will not hold the boards together. You should put at least two nails in each corner. Now make another rectangle just like this one. One will be for the front of the stand, and the other for the back.

Next, you'll need to connect the front to the back using the 2' long boards. Look at Figure 2. The top connecting boards need to sit on top of the frames at the very ends. Be very careful because, at this point, the frame is not very stable. Hammer two nails into each corner.

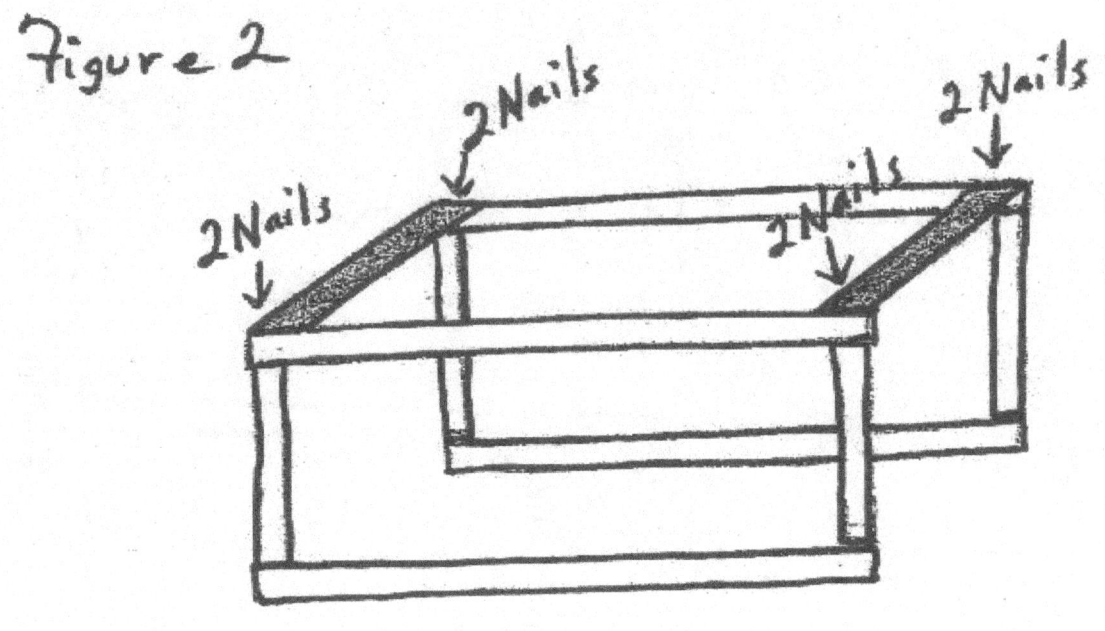

Figure 2

2 Nails
2 Nails
2 Nails
2 Nails

Now, look at Figure 3. Place the two remaining 2' long boards on the bottom of the frame, as shown. They should rest on top of the bottom of it, just inside the end boards. Again, hammer two nails on each end of each board, as shown.

Figure 3

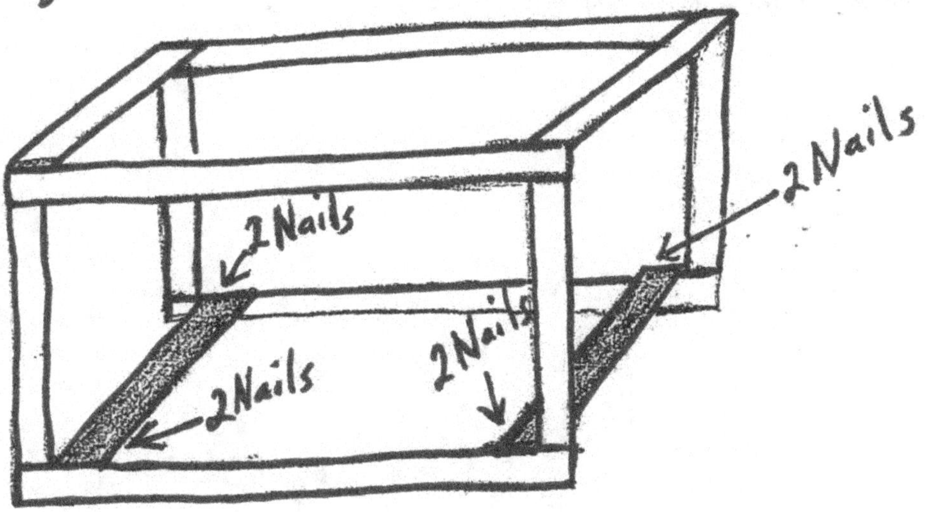

The stand is a little sturdier now, but still not sturdy enough to put any weight on it. To stabilize it, you'll need to attach the front panel and the side panels.

For the front panel, you'll need a piece of plywood that is approximately 4' long and 2' 9" wide. Be sure to measure carefully, and always measure twice to make sure the measurement is correct. If the measurement is not right, you'll cut your board wrong and it won't fit correctly. Once again, you can cut the plywood with a hand saw, or you can have your parent or a grown-up cut it for you with an electric saw. Never try to use the electric saw yourself.

Now, look at Figure 4. Lay the frame down on its back. Place the front panel on top of the frame. Make sure the top of the panel lines up even with the top of the frame. Also make sure the panel lines up with the sides. Nail it, as shown.

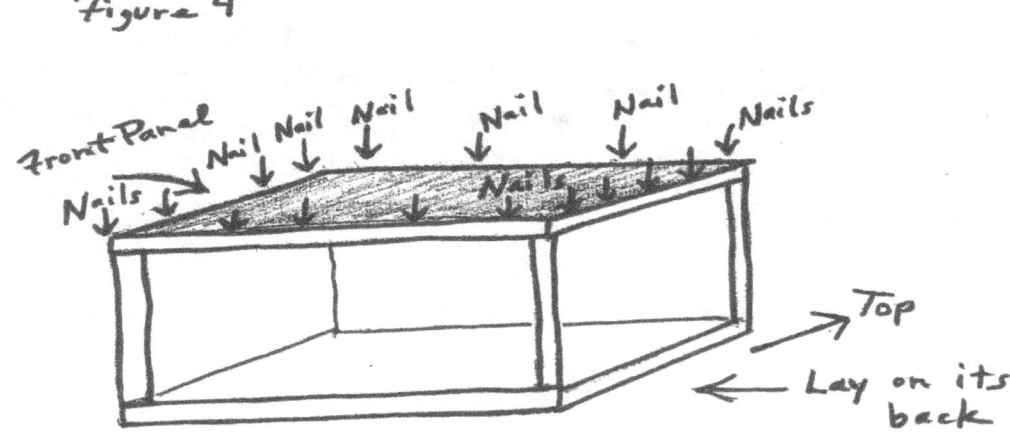

Figure 4

You can use shorter nails for the panels, since they aren't as thick as the 2x4s. You can use 1" or 1 ½" nails. They should be long enough to hold the panel on securely. Hammer the nails all around the outside of the frame, placing at least four nails on each side. You can always put more nails in it, but you should have <u>at least</u> four on each side. Okay, now you can stand the frame back up. You're ready to put the end panels on it.

For the ends, you'll need two (2) pieces of plywood, each one 2' wide and 2' 9" tall. Again, measure very carefully before cutting the wood. Use only the hand saw if you're cutting it yourself.

Now, look at Figure 5. Place one end panel on the end of the frame. Be sure to line up the top of the panel with the top of the frame. You should have someone hold the board in place while you hammer a couple of nails into it. Be sure to use the shorter nails and put at least four of them along each edge of the panel.

Figure 5

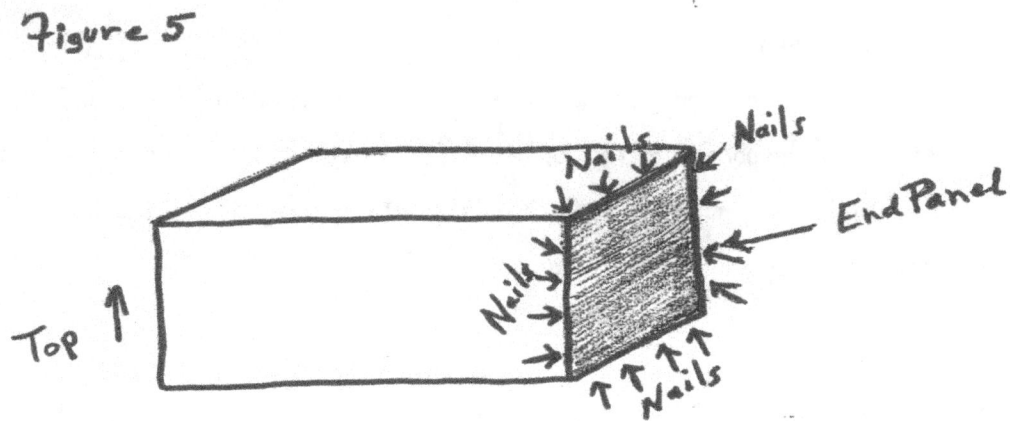

Okay, now put the other end panel on the same way. It's beginning to look like a lemonade stand!!

Now look at Figure 6.

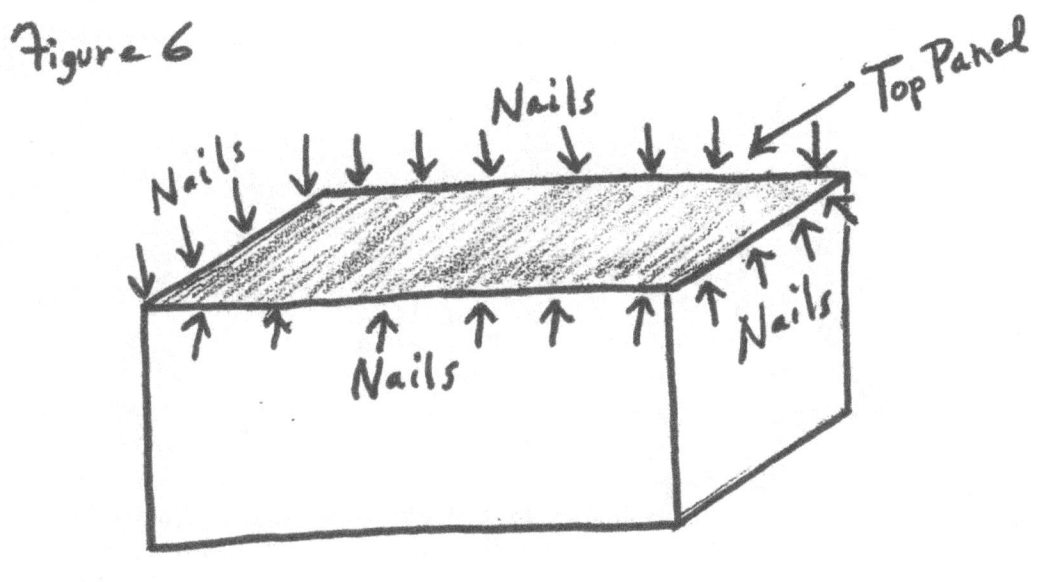

Figure 6

Nails

Top Panel

Nails

Nails

Nails

For the top of the stand (the table part), you'll need one more piece of plywood, or a board, that is 4' long and about 2 ½' wide. After the board is cut, lay it on top of the frame, making sure that it lines up on both ends. Let the board hang over the front of the frame a little. Now nail it into place, using the shorter nails. Be sure to put at least four nails on each end, and probably more than four on the front and back sides.

Now your base is complete. It should be sturdy enough to hold your lemonade pitcher and glasses, along with whatever other goodies you'll decide to sell. However, it's probably *not* sturdy enough to sit on!

If you want to add a sign to your custom-built stand, you can do so fairly easily. You'll need two boards about 5 feet long each. They should be small, thin boards. Next, for the sign itself, you'll need a piece of lightweight plywood about 4' long and 8" high. If you want, you can use a piece of cardboard for the sign part. Lay the boards on the ground as shown in Figure 7.

Figure 7

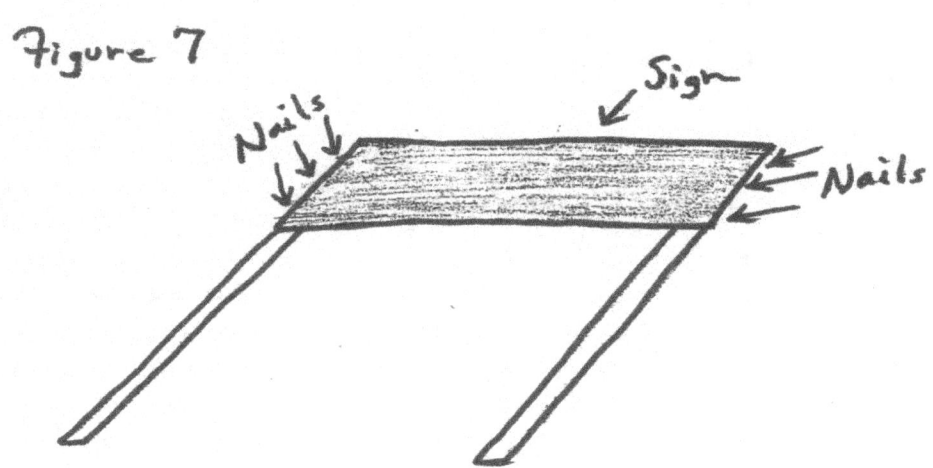

Nail the sign panel to the long boards, making sure that the sides of the panel line up straight with the boards. Then, carefully raise the sign section up and stand it in front of the base of your stand. See Figure 8. Nail the long boards securely to the front of the base. Be sure the front of the sign panel will face your customers.

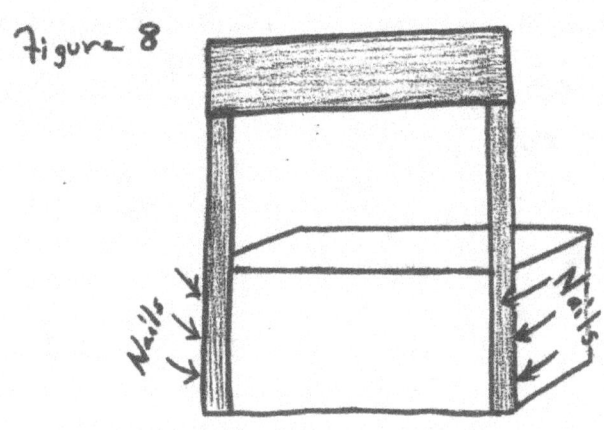

Figure 8

When everything is all nailed together, carefully look it all over to make sure that all the boards are still nailed together tightly. If anything is coming loose, you'll need to re-nail them, especially the sign section. You certainly don't want your sign falling on a customer's head—even if it is just cardboard!

After the stand is all built, you can paint it if you want to. Or, you can leave it unpainted. How you decorate it is up to you. You might remember, though, that if you plan on keeping the stand for awhile, the wood parts will last longer if you paint them.

Don't forget to paint the sign section! You can write "Lemonade" on it or you can write the name of your business on it, such as "Stop and Sip." You can put your prices up there, if you want. However, if you decide to change your price, you'll have to change your sign. So, you may not want to paint the price up there. Remember that you can paint your sign before you nail it to the base, if it would be easier.

Also, you can paint a sign on the front of the base and even on the sides if you want. It's your stand---fix it up the way you want your business to look.

Okay, as you can see, there are a lot of different ways to set up or to build a lemonade stand. Pick out the one that is best for you. It can be as simple and easy as a cardboard box or as customized as you want it to be. The stand is your "store." Now, let's get to your "product."

CHAPTER FOUR: MAKING THE LEMONADE

To have a successful business, you MUST have a good product! Your product is what you sell---your lemonade. Oh, sure, people will buy your lemonade whether it is good or not, at least once. But, if it's not good…..if it doesn't satisfy their thirst….. if it doesn't make them smile and want more…….then they won't be coming back for another cup. And it's very important to keep them coming back! So, let's think about what kind of lemonade you want to sell.

Lots of folks like the good "old-fashioned" lemonade. It's what we'll call the homemade kind---made from ingredients like lemons and sugar. It's probably the best tasting, but it takes a little more work than some of the other types of lemonade.   The best things in life usually do take a little more work. There are many different ways to make it. Here's one recipe that's simple and easy to follow:

GOOD OLD-FASHIONED LEMONADE

(Makes 1 gallon)

Ingredients:

8-12 Lemons

2 ½ cups of Sugar

1 Gallon Water

Roll the lemons back and forth on the top of a table using the palm of your hand to soften them. The softer they are, the more juice you'll be able to get out of them. Then cut the lemons in half and squeeze the juice out of them into a gallon jar. Squeeze out all you can. If you have a lemon juicer, you can use it. It's okay if you get some of the pulp (the little bitty pieces of lemon fruit) into the jar. Actually the lemonade is better if it has pulp in it. The pulp adds a lot of lemon flavor to it. You can use any number of lemons, but I suggest at least eight. If you want it to be very sour, you can use up to twelve lemons.

After you get all the lemons squeezed and can't get any more juice out of them, slowly stir the sugar into the jar. Stir it up until all the sugar is dissolved, or melted, into the juice. It may take a little while for it all to dissolve.

Now, carefully pour the water into the lemon juice and sugar mixture. Stir until it's all mixed together. (Remember to always add the sugar to the lemon juice **before** you add the water.) There you have it---fresh, homemade old-fashioned lemonade!

Fill a glass with ice cubes and pour the lemonade over the ice. Now, try it yourself to make sure it tastes okay. You may need to add a little sugar if it's not sweet enough. But, remember, lemonade is supposed to be sour, so don't get it too sweet. If you do get it too sweet, though, you can always add more lemon juice.

This recipe makes about a gallon of lemonade. If you don't want to make that much, cut the recipe in half to make half a gallon (2 quarts). Just use half of the ingredients (4-6 lemons, 1 ¼ cup of sugar, and half a gallon of water).

Okay, now another way to make lemonade is to use the frozen kind. It's a little easier to make than the "homemade" kind, but can be just as tasty.

FROZEN LEMONADE

(Makes about 2 quarts or ½ gallon)

1 can frozen Lemonade

3 ½ cans of cold Water

All you have to do is open the can and dump it into a pitcher. If you let the can sit out of the freezer for a little while (about 30 minutes), the lemonade inside will soften and will be easier to come out of the can. Now add about 3 ½ cans of cold water to the pitcher. Read the instructions on the side of the lemonade can for the exact amount of water to add. Different brands of lemonade require different amounts of water. Stir the lemonade and water until all the lemonade is mixed in and it is no longer frozen. Now it's ready to be poured over ice and enjoyed. Easy, huh?

To add more lemon flavor to it, you can slice up a lemon and place the slices in the bottom of the pitcher. Then put the frozen lemonade in and mash it all up together. When the frozen lemonade is no longer frozen and the lemons are all mashed, then add the water.

Another way to make lemonade is with a package of lemonade-flavored Kool-Aid. It's also easy to make.

KOOL-AID LEMONADE

(Makes 2 quarts)

1 Package Lemonade-flavored Kool-Aid (unsweetened)

1 cup Sugar

2 quarts Water

Simply mix the Kool-Aid and the sugar together in a 2-quart pitcher. Then stir in the water and mix thoroughly until all is dissolved. That's all you have to do. You can also mash lemon slices in this kind of lemonade for a more flavorful drink. As a matter of fact, you can mash them into any kind of lemonade you make.

You'll need to try all these recipes and figure out which one will be the one you'll want to sell to your customers. You can even switch back and forth until you figure out which one is the most popular with them. Once you decide, though, try to stick with it because your repeat customers will be coming back for the kind of lemonade that they've already tasted and liked.

One other way to make lemonade is by using a combination of both "old-fashioned" ingredients and the frozen kind. It really has a lot of flavor to it, is easy to make, and is sure to get you a lot of compliments. Try it yourself:

DELICIOUS COMBO LEMONADE

1 can of frozen Lemonade (6 oz)

1 cup Sugar

1 Lemon

7 cups cold Water

Slice the lemon up very thin and put the slices in a 2-quart pitcher. Add the sugar and mash it into the lemon slices until the sugar is dissolved and the lemon is very juicy. Then add the frozen lemonade and the cold water. Stir it all up together until the lemonade is no longer frozen. Pour it over ice and try it. When you pour the lemonade into a glass, try to get a piece of the mashed lemon in the glass. That will give it lots of flavor.

Now, if you want to make the lemonade you see "extra special," there are some little extras that you can do. Try putting a slice of lemon in each cup or try sticking a slice that you've notched on one side on the rim of the cup.

Or you can add a little bit of grated lemon rind (it's called the "zest" of the lemon) to whichever recipe you make. Just grate a little of the bright yellow part of the peel into your mixture (use an extra lemon for this and grate it off while the lemon is whole). Make sure that you grate it up very fine. You don't want clumps of it in your lemonade. If you don't have a grater, try using a potato peeler. Have your mom or dad show you how to use it.

Be very careful with it because it has a very sharp edge on it. Be sure to just peel off the yellow part of the rind. You don't want the white part (it usually is bitter).

Another way to make your lemonade a little different from everyone else's, is to slice up one of your lemons instead of squeezing it. Cut it into thin slices and lay the slices in the bottom of your pitcher. Then add the sugar. Then mash the lemon slices and sugar all together with a wooden spoon or a masher. Keep mashing them until all the sugar is dissolved and the lemon slices are very juicy. Then add the lemon juice you've squeezed out of the other lemons and the water and stir it all up thoroughly. If you don't sell all your lemonade that same day, you might want to remove the lemon rinds because they'll make your lemonade bitter the next day, if you don't.

If you want to make "pink" old-fashioned lemonade, try adding a few drops of grape juice or beet juice to the pitcher. Don't add too much, though, or you'll have red lemonade and a weird flavor. Also, if you're using the frozen lemonade or Kool-Aid lemonade methods, those can both be purchased in "pink."

So, there you have it-a few basic ways to make lemonade. There are many, many more ways, but these are the easy ones. One tip to remember is to **always** add the sugar to the lemon juice before you add the water!

Now-something that's very important! Making the lemonade can get a little messy sometimes. Whatever you do-no matter what kind you decide to make-**always** clean up the mess as soon as possible. If you use your mom's kitchen, I would suggest that you clean it up before you take your lemonade out to your stand. That way, she won't have to clean it up and she'll be happy to let you use her kitchen the next time. If you leave it messy, she might not want to let you make any more lemonade. And-remember-if you start selling a lot of your lemonade, you're going to be "making" a lot of it. So, always leave your work area clean-whether it's in the kitchen, on the back porch, or at the stand itself.

Okay, as soon as you get your lemonade made, be sure to cover the pitcher with a lid or some plastic wrap, if you don't have a lid. That way, little pests (like flies or gnats) won't get in it. When you're outside, they have a way of finding stuff that has sugar in it.

Now, you're ready to start selling. But before you do, you'll need to decide if you're going to have more than one size of cup to offer your customers. Of course, you'll want to charge more for the larger cups if you do. Also, you'll need to have something to store ice in. A good ice chest will keep your ice from melting. And, speaking of ice, are you going to buy it by the bag, or use ice cubes out of your refrigerator? If you sell a lot of lemonade, you may run out of ice. So, you should always have extra ice available if you need it. Maybe you can store up cubes in your freezer, or have an extra bag or two in there.

All right-with all that said-let's get to the selling part!

CHAPTER FIVE: ATTRACTING CUSTOMERS

How do you let people know about your stand? Of course, if you set the stand up in your front yard, your neighbors will see it, but what about the people on the next block? And what about your friends? You can tell the ones you see or talk to, but what about the ones you don't see all the time? And what about people you don't know? You'll need to advertise!

What does advertising mean? It means to tell others about your business-to let them know about what you're selling and where you're selling it.

You could put an ad in the newspaper, but that costs money. Luckily, there are many ways to advertise for free.

One easy way is to make up some flyers that tell about your business. You can make them with just sheets of paper and a magic marker. Or, if you're a computer whiz, you can make up flyers on your PC. You can make the flyers as simple as you want, or you can make them as fancy as you want. Black ink on white paper will do, but red ink on neon green paper might get a lot more notice. Or, you may prefer crayons and poster board. Or maybe you'll just want to put up big arrows all over the neighborhood, pointing the way to your stand. It's all up to you. It's always good, though, to use whatever you have around the house (be sure to ask permission if it's not yours). That way, you won't have to "invest" money in buying materials for flyers.

The most important thing about flyers is what you write on them. And you really don't need to say anything more than what you're selling and where you're selling it. You don't have to mention the price-as a matter of fact, it's probably better if you don't. You want people to come try your product, and once they are there and see that ice-cold glass of delicious lemonade, they'll be happy to pay the price you're asking. You might mention something on your flyers like "Ask about our Special." You can then run "specials," like half-price sales or buy-one-get-one-free.

Another important thing is where you put your flyers. Where should you put them? Tack or tape them up wherever people will see them-on a fence post, on a tree, in a store window, at the school, at the Laundromat, or at the ball field. Ask your friends to help you. If you make up a lot of flyers, you can hand them out to people you see on the sidewalk or at the grocery store or at the ball park. You can pass them out at school or put them under the windshields of cars in a parking lot.

If you do want to make up a lot of flyers, you don't have to write them all by hand. Just make up one good one and then get copies made of it. You can use a computer to make the copies, but it will use up a lot of your ink cartridge. You may be able to talk your mom or dad or maybe a neighbor into making copies for you where they work. Or, if they're not allowed to do that, you can pay to have some printed up at a copy shop. It will cost you a little money, but it will be worth it if you don't have to write up all the flyers yourself. You might even talk the people at the copy shop into making you a deal since you're a kid. Like, you could tell them that if they will give you 100 copies for free, you'll give them a free lemonade every day that your stand is open!

Now, after you get your flyers make, decide where you want to put them or pass them out, and then get permission to do it before you do. If you don't know who to get permission from, then either find out or put them somewhere else. Remember, too, that you should never leave flyers where they will become litter.

If your neighborhood has a newsletter, you can ask to put an announcement in it about your lemonade stand. Write up something like this:

Now open for the summer!

STOP 'N SIP LEMONADE

114 North Oak

Ask about our Specials!

Another way to attract customers is to put up flags or streamers around your stand. They will "draw attention" to it. Of course, this only works if there are people within sight of it. It will work really well, though, if your stand is among trees, or behind a car or something, and not easily visible at first glance. The streamers or flags waving in the breeze will tell people to look your way.

Still another way to attract customers is with balloons. If you get helium balloons, you can fly them high over your stand. Bright yellow balloons with lemons drawn on them would be a good way to advertise!

Yet another way to get customers is to set up your stand close to a big garage sale or an event that will have a lot of people coming to it. If you do choose to set up your stand at a temporary location, such as a garage sale, don't forget to hand out your flyers, telling your customers where your stand is usually located. That way, when they want more of your delicious lemonade, they'll know where to find you.

CHAPTER SIX: KEEP THEM COMING BACK FOR MORE!

In order to have a good business, you have to have "repeat" customers. That means that you have to keep them coming back--time after time--for more of your wonderful lemonade.

How do you do that? First, you have to have good-tasting lemonade, which we've already talked about in Chapter Four. If it's not good, they won't want to buy it from you anymore. But......if it is good or even better than good.....they will be back for more. Secondly, you have to give them "good service." What does that mean? It means you have to be nice to them. Be police, be friendly, and be honest. Go out of your way to do the little extras--like maybe give them a straw with their cup, or offer them a place to sit while they're sipping on their drink. Chit chat with them about how their day is going, or about the weather, or maybe "What's your dog's name?" (if they have a dog with them)--anything to make them feel comfortable and want to come back. Also, sometimes if you keep them talking, they may stand there and drink all their lemonade and want another glass while they are there. However, that might not be a good thing if you're giving free refills that day.

Be careful, though, about letting too many of your friends hang out at your place of business. Sometimes, if there's a crowd there or too many rowdy kids, people may decide to go somewhere else to quench their thirst. So, let your friends know that it's a business-- they are welcome to buy lemonade (tell them you won't make a profit if you give it to them for free). If they still want to hang around, put them to work handing out flyers or going out telling people where your stand is. Hopefully, they'll get the message that your business is important to you.

Another way to keep your customers coming back for more is to run "Specials." That means something that you don't do all the time, but just do at certain times or on certain days. As I've already mentioned, some ideas for "Specials" you may run are giving your customers one free refill, or giving them the second glass of lemonade for half price. Or, you may want to offer them "Two glasses for the price of one!" These "Specials" are things that you can put on your signs to attract people to your stand.

Also, you can keep customers coming back for more by making your stand attractive to them. An attractive stand will help people remember you and your lemonade. Make sure your stand and the area around it is always clean and free of trash. Keep a little wastebasket or cardboard box next to the stand for people to put their empty cups in. Always keep the counter top wiped off. Sticky spots attract ants, and that's not something you want to keep coming back!

So, if you offer a good product (yummy lemonade) and good service (polite and helpful), and have a neat and clean stand, people will enjoy buying lemonade from you—not just once, but over and over.

CHAPTER SEVEN: KEEPING TRACK OF YOUR MONEY

It's very important that you keep track of the money you spend for supplies and the money you make from sales. Grown-ups call this "accounting." If you do, you'll know how much "profit" you make.

What is profit? Profit is what's left over after you pay for your ingredients if you have to buy them (like lemons and sugar), your supplies (like cups and straws), your advertising (like the cost to make copies of your flyers, if you pay someone to do it), and your payroll (what you pay your friends to help you). Anything left over is money you've made—pure profit!! Bucks in the bank!! The goal of any business is to make as much profit as it can. Sure, it will be fun anyway, even if you don't make any money. But wouldn't it be nice to buy that new bike or that computer game you've been wanting? Sure it would!!

Okay, the first thing you'll need to get is a money box. Your money box is simply whatever you keep your money in. It can be a cigar box or a Tupperware bowl with a lid. Or, if you have one, you can use a metal box with a lock on it. It doesn't really matter what you keep it in, as long as the money will be safe there. Never leave the box unattended. If you have to go into the house for something, take it with you. That way, you won't risk letting someone walk off with all your profits!

Start off each day with a little money in your box. Don't leave it all in there.....just enough to make change with. Someone may pay for their fifty-cent lemonade with a one-dollar bill, so you'll need some quarters in your box. If someone pays with a five-dollar bill, you'll need some one-dollar bills in order to give them their change back.

You'll need enough change for the first few customers, or until people have paid you enough quarters to allow you to make change for others. How much is enough? You probably won't know until you see about how many customers you're going to have or how much lemonade you're going to sell. To be on the safe side, I'd say to at least start out with two or three dollars in change. If someone only has a dollar bill and you don't have any change, try to talk them into buying two lemonades. Maybe they can take one home to their mom or give one to a friend. Or, tell them they can come back and drink the second one tomorrow.

Now, if someone needs change for a five-dollar bill, you'll need to also have some one-dollar bills in your money box. If you have to, you can borrow some from your parents or a friend, and then pay them back at the end of the day. Always pay them back quickly.

That way, you'll have "good credit" with them, and they will be more likely to loan you something the next time you need it.

If someone wants to buy a lemonade, but gives you a large bill (like a ten or a twenty, or maybe even a five) that you don't have change for, be sure to tell them that you don't have enough change. Sometimes, they may have a smaller bill or enough change in their pocket to pay you. If they don't, you'll need to decide if the customer can pay you later or if he needs to go get change before you give him his lemonade.

To keep track of your money, I suggest that you keep a written record of it. You'll need to keep track of not only what you take in, but also of what you spend. Your "accounting form" can be quite simple, or it can be more complicated. It's up to you.

For a simple record, just keep track of how much you spend (your expenses) and how much you make (your income). Then all you will need to do to find out how much "profit" you make will be to subtract your expenses from your income.

Now if you want to keep a more detailed record of your business, you can keep track of the different kind of expenses you have and the different kinds of income you make. For example, your expenses might be divided into money spent on building the stand, money spent on ingredients for the lemonade, money spent on supplies, money spent on advertising, and money paid to your helpers.

Your income might be divided into the number of large cups of lemonade you sold, the number of small cups that you sold, the number of large refills, the number of small refills, etc. You get the idea!

At the end of each day, tally up your profit. Just add up all the money you made (your income) and add up everything you had to spend for that day (your expenses). Then just subtract your expenses from your income. That's your profit!

Also, be sure to keep track of any money that you may have to borrow from other people, so that you can pay them back at the end of the day.

Of course, you don't <u>have</u> to keep track of everything. But, it is a good idea. It lets you know if you're really making any money, or if maybe you need to cut back on expenses, or maybe if you need to try to sell more lemonade! Try it, at least! It's a great way to show what a smart business person you are!!

****

Okay – there you have it – how to start your own lemonade business! So plan what you're going to do, choose a name, build a stand, mix your lemonade, advertise your business, and sell all you can! Now get busy and have fun!!

Other Books by D J Parry

<u>The Gift of Christmas</u>

Stephen, Thomas, and Amy all grew up loving Christmas...not just the day itself, but all the fun and activities that led up to it. Stephen loved it so much that he started The Christmas Club, which shared many secret activities aimed at getting people to believe. Then one day, everything changes. What happens next is a story that you will not soon forget.

<u>https://www.amazon.com/author/djparry</u>

www.ingramcontent.com/pod-product-compliance
Lightning Source LLC
Chambersburg PA
CBHW081402170526

45166CB00010B/3179